PRAISE FOR

Maker of Heaven &:

"These poems seek the name inside each living thing, the song inside the song, the story inside the story, and a belonging deeper than race, gender, class, and even species. When Jason Myers' vision penetrates the body and finds the laws that manifest the body, when he sees through our human history, recent and ancient, and discovers older imperatives at war and in harmony, the reader feels sometimes troubled by his hard-won revelations of human nature, consistently surprised by the courage, the understanding, and the beauty of his process, and finally grateful for having been granted such sight."

—**Li-Young Lee, Winner of the
William Carlos Williams Award**

"The poems in Jason Myers' debut collection, *Maker of Heaven &*, at once grasp at and let go, approach and surrender, engaging the very gestures of the religious life, carving the path of the seeker. Vast, they contain multitudes: 'What is all around me, the past, the air, the lone pear on a tree in need of company, I absorb, & what is within me spools out into the day . . . like breath, like a song.' These are praise songs from a true believer, a priest, and they meet our precarious moment and transcend, cracking meaning out of experience and rending blessings from everyday life."

—**Carrie Fountain,
Former Poet Laureate of Texas**

"*Maker of Heaven &* is a book of wonder, and in it Jason Myers suggests that what we wonder can indeed be made into art as God must have felt wonder when making the cosmos: 'There was a secret / name inside every living thing, / a song underneath every song.' Each of these poems seems rooted in a belief in 'brutal brotherly love.' These poems are a testament to a poet's faith in the word."

—**Jericho Brown, Winner of the
Pulitzer Prize for Poetry**

Jason Myers

Maker of Heaven &

For J.D.,
with appreciation & affection.
&&&

BELLE
POINT
PRESS

Fort Smith, Arkansas

MAKER OF HEAVEN &

Cover image: *Baptism* by Lanecia Rouse Tinsley
Photography by Hailie Durrett

Edited by Casie Dodd
Design & typography by Belle Point Press

Belle Point Press
Fort Smith, Arkansas
bellepointpress.com
editor@bellepointpress.com

Printed in the United States of America

27 26 25 24 23   1 2 3 4 5

ISBN: 979-8-9858965-9-6

MH&/BPP9

I taste in my natural appetite
the bond of live things everywhere.

—Lucille Clifton, "cutting greens"

Sometimes you will feel, like nothing else, the sweet, electric drowse of creation.

—Mary Oliver, "Sand Dabs, Seven"

THE BODY OF CHRIST

IN THE BEGINNING

How to Make a Sound

Luke 1

There was a time, like Zechariah,
I did not believe I'd become a father.
We had waited, my wife & I, & waited,

& waited some more.

I wasn't forced into silence
the way Zechariah was, no angel
condemned me for my pride, my want
of knowledge.

We had plenty in our lack.

What knowledge would I have desired anyway?

One day, after months of frozen dinners & cheap wine,
binged series after binged series,

a child arrived.

His mother placed him in my wife's arms, then mine.

The night before, after margaritas
& restless scanning of the starless sky,
I had fallen into a sleep so dark
the dream that came wrecked me awake.

An expanse of grass as omnivorous as the ocean, & way
out at the edge of the horizon, a horse.
Maybe not a horse. Maybe an old man
bent by years of hauling his life from one meeting to the next.

His life. His life. His very life.
I tried to call to the creature on the horizon,
to say *you there, I know you, I see you*,
but, as in many dreams, I had no voice.

So, when I held, for the first time,
our son,
what slipped from my mouth was
part cry, part spill of almost verb, a word
like *love*, insufficient, immeasurable, & perfect.

BROODING

When I put my mouth to my son's nose,
is ours like YHWH's intimacy with Adam?

Strange, God started not with a baby
but an adult male.

When asked about his childhood, Adam looked toward the horizon,
blank blank blank,

& hoped his inquisitors would interpret his silence for a meaning
richer than he could achieve with words.

Before he was born, my son, I watched mothers
feed babies, mouths at nipples, nipples dripping the need

of one body into the need of another body,
amazed at the porous boundaries of our being.

Now my amazement has something folded into it,
call it longing, as I call most feelings I can't identify,

or anguish, that cousin of amazement that lurks
inside each breath to remind us of breath's brevity.

This chiaroscuro of affection & the something that shades it—
oh, call it brooding, as Jesus said of how he wanted

to gather Jerusalem unto him. I picture his body
all nipple

& the mouths, my mouth, sucking, crying out in hunger,
being fed &, after being fed, still wanting satisfaction.

I want to transmit something of my being to my son,
to be a liquid I might pour into him.

Though I did not give him life, I give him life.

Imperfect Gods

Genesis 1:26

In a dream Tomas asks
how much my faith hinges
on the idea of a perfect
God. I think of Elohim saying
let us make humankind
in our image, after our
likeness. How many gods
were there that day?
What about elbows, one suggested
to the scornful laughter
of the others. *Let's give them*
such yearning that no
quantity of affection shall
quench. *Secretions*, another
proposed. *Did you say*
secrets, the hearing-impaired
gods asked. *Those, too.*
Nipples, the horniest god
insisted. *Memory*, one
lonely god, with a hesitant,
loss-layered voice, offered.
Ah, that's a good one, the
favored god, the beauty,
responded, gazing over
the ropey, crenellated cosmos.
As they argued over body
parts & the location of
the soul, what effect
time would have on all
this, one small planet
began to produce, without

direction or approval,
a field of lupine, & around
their colorful collars swarmed
a host of bees, their coats
thick with striped sweetness,
the wisdom of the pasture.
They'll ruin it, a cynical
god opined, & the gods,
none too keen on clarity
or communication, didn't
bother to ask what would
be ruined, by whom. Wind,
from a warehouse the gods
of logistics had neglected,
began to move over an alliance
of water one god wanted to name
the deep, while another
held fast to *ocean*. *Would
you look at that*, the oldest
god, a gregarious crank,
whispered. Thus, they continued
to work out the universe,
strangeness by strangeness,
never quite satisfied.

NEARER MY GOD

In the oak-dark darkness becoming
light under the phosphorous exclamations of a magnolia tree
three men work.
They solder steel, sparks amber & orange shoot & spit
& hang, for the briefest moment, little bits
of fire on the now-blue, now-gray air.
It's cold out there, on the other side
of the windows.

In here, in the hospital cafeteria,
I'm eating spinach & eggs when
two women at the table next to mine
begin to pray.

I hear that sweet name, Jesus, sail
the lake of their lips,
& every few seconds
one or the other
raises an affirmation
'Yesss
Yehhhssss
here three measures,
here more.

They are reassuring God.

They are rocking
a baby to sleep
the words slip
out & over the room & sing,
Mary's arms wrapped

around her boy,
first an infant
delicate & unfathomable as those on the NICU,
then a man
covered in blood
like the woman
on the gurney
in the trauma bay
who'd been bludgeoned
about the face
by her boyfriend's
baseball bat.

I don't know
who these women are
praying for
but I will take
their Yehhhhhss
word become chant become river
of sound
sound most close to silence
near to music
nearer my God to thee
I will take it, Lord,
spread it across
my day
my life
like balm
like globes of fire
soldering us together.

Spies

Numbers 13

This morning I watched a hummingbird
steal secrets from the pansies I bought
at Home Depot, ransom them to the roses.
My privacy settings are out of date. *Unless*
a grain of wheat falls into the earth…
Our dog is dying. The day we adopted him,
when we swore we were going
just to look, we walked
around the base of Stone Mountain,
where laser lights flatter Jefferson
Davis, King's dream dead. *The Lord*
said to Moses, 'Send men to spy out
the land of Canaan.' We are told
it was *the season of the first ripe grapes.*
How long does it take land to decide
who belongs? How long before you know
a promise is kept or broken? *Promise*
you won't die, we'd say to Gilbert
before we knew he was sick. Secrets
circle his eyes like birds wondering
is that my nest, is that my nest? The spies
took a single cluster of grapes, some
pomegranates & figs. I hate the hard
work of pomegranates, the agony
of each small hour of juice, time
in its endless divisions. *I may not get*
there with you, King said in Memphis,
there being Canaan, or wherever nectar
like water, like water flowed. How
many of his wires had been tapped,
Hoover convinced he was a communist

spy. How else to explain such vehement
displays of love, such oracles of
justice? When I say *nectar*, I mean
clean water, affordable housing, nobody
calling the police. Much rabbinical wisdom
suggests the language of Torah
is entirely code, an encryption
of divine lusciousness in each
woozy vowel, patient consonant.
Now, I write, *I can hold his dear*
face in my hands. Someday, though,
these will just be words. Every tongue
is a temple of ghosts. When cells
cross wires we call it cancer. When
night slips into night we call it
holy matrimony. The sounds of
heaven & the sounds of ache echo.
In Exodus, YHWH responds only
when the people cry out. Like we need
to know lack to know love. Like a body
out of tune learns a lighter melody. To
wander from piedmont to piedmont
is to revere, right or wrong, the summit.
Today's ripeness is tomorrow's rot.
Yesterday my empty hands held such promise,
such promise.

On the Other Side of Robert E. Lee

I go with a friend to Barton Springs
where another friend
in 1958
asked the city to allow her friends to swim.
Does water know when the body in it
has skin has blood has a history of
being told no does the air that Eric
Garner that Sandra Bland could
not breathe say oh these lungs are
the good lungs of a worthy one?
Where is the past & what does it
weigh? Who decided to name
the road that does not cross Town
Lake, Cesar Chavez, Martin Luther
King after a man who was
so many say a mere product of his times
whose likeness Episcopalians
stained in glass next to Jesus
on the campus where Draylen
Mason might have continued
his mastery of the upright bass
of which Mingus said
making the simple complicated
is commonplace; making the
complicated simple, that's creative.
At the church where I met my friend,
founded by her mother & her mother's
friends in 1941 when they could
not drink from certain fountains
or find room at any Episcopal
inn, we do not have stained

glass but large windows that
allow us to see the disfigured
religioning world turn from
dust to wet flames of wild
flowers back to dust while
the liturgy of time pours
ice cold water over our im-
perfect implicated heads.

Oral History of Insatiability

I woke in the wreck of history
still drowsy, a dryness in my
bed, my bones. *Would you*
like fingers, the Lord asked,
& gave me plenty. There was
no music, no garden in them.
I wanted to be touched the way
I had touched, delicately, but
with great passion. *If you want*
another kind of lover, Leonard
Cohen crooned. *Not my will*,
Martin Luther King intoned,
but God's. I wanted a word
for every surface, for the belly
& the underbelly, the line between
the lines. There was a secret
name inside every living thing,
a song underneath every song.
What happened then, I asked,
meaning both *before* & *next*.
The Lord said *Kabul*. Said

manifest destiny. Said *Rembrandt*
said *Bordeaux* said *Dakota*
said *Chelsea Hotel* said *Egyptian*
cotton said *Homer.* The Greek
poet, I asked. *No. Homer Plessy.*
Oh, I said. *I see.* But I did not.
Lulls, curtains, continuations.
You want company, the Lord asked,
& made New Orleans, oceans,
rye bread, Cointreau. There
were some companions sent
by another party. There were
days smothered in solitude,
nights when I thought, *if only*
*I could sleep, if only...*but I
could not complete the sentence.
Are you hungry, the Lord asked.
Oh my. Oh yes. Oh my yes.

MOTHERLAND

My mother was born in a country
I can't pronounce. Sometimes she
forgets my birthday, calls me by a
different name. My mother remembers
every shadow in the forest, each bird's
appeal. I am from her, & from someplace
else. My mother traveled by herself
before I was born, collected apologies
& folk songs. She writes in lovelorn ink.
In dialogue with winter, who never
knows what to say. I'm a reluctant
citizen. Think of all the flowers, my
mother says before sleep. Dahlia,
foxglove, feverfew. Chop, chop.
When we've been separated—by lakes,
by days—a nostalgia, like a film,
forms between us, clouding what
we see. I know my heart is small
& has no place in history. The loaves
of sourdough, the expensive whiskey.
Another cake, another candle. I see
the effects of grief in the hair graying
her head. Sometimes when I think
I'm looking straight ahead, it's the past,
haunted-house mirror held before
my frightened face. Everything
closer than it appears. Intimacy, awful
intimacy. People I meet along the way
tell me of their mothers. Who taught
them the secrets of thread & needle,
how much garlic to add to any dish.

Who gave them their scents, the songs
that come when skin encounters the
strange mist of company. O mother of
blue, mother of dawn. Nights I spent
weeping on trains, leather watch-band
sealed to wrist, I couldn't tell one month
from the next, or when we'd crossed
a border—only that the war was still on.

PHILADELPHIA

The day I was born
Ronald Reagan stood
a few miles from where
James Chaney, Andrew
Goodman, & Michael
Schwerner were murdered
sixteen years prior
for trying to register
black people to vote.
Said he believed
in states' rights.
I see their faces:
Michael, 24, killed
first, his bulletsmocked
eyes, & Andrew, 20,
a nice Jewish kid down
south to study anthropology
& boy did he get some, &,
finally, horribly, James,
21, chain-whipped across
his smart mouth, *imago dei*.
What of their rights
to live   to yearn
for other bodies
to sit with comfort
& care near their own,
to hear trumpets not
pitched to war or mourning
but in the sheer elation
of brassy sensuality—
the groove, the vamp,

the blue note, the red.
When I celebrate my birth
I feel the pleasure
& pain of circumstance:
every word, every right,
the passage of time & laws
in this land, this place of
brutal brotherly love
·swirled around my long
white body like a swarm
of bees, buzzing, honey-
hounded, & dangerous.

LET THERE BE

Imago Dei

in the image of want
in the image of tenderly, tenderly, the awakening of juice in the
joints of the dogwood, her
winterleft sheet music sifted into scores of again when last
we saw she knew no flowers
in the image of the fur that garlands a peach, how it anticipates &
delays sweetness
in the image of Christ
in the image of looking at woods that have not yet been cleared
knowing they will be
in the image of someone who, having decided, after much agonizing
uncertainty,
to move to a new house, must be hospitalized on the day
of the move when,
from anxiety or other heartache, she trips while carrying
a box to the U-Haul, her
temple rent by the rock where she had, on many
sunstalled afternoons, lazed with
her golden retriever, dead four years
in the image of larkspurs & larks & lurk late & the woman who
wrote lurk late in a poem
& the man who wrote poems in the castle of his whiteness
& uttered his arrogance
when that woman won a prize
in the image of history's broken shoulder
in the image of creek
in the image of whatever feeling the word creek evokes, memories
luscious & wounding, the
water, the water, its purple vocation

in the image of feathers, oh my pretty, & petals, & the talk of rain as
            it licks its fingers & gets
            down to the business of fucking everything
in the image of animals bred & crossbred & cornfed & queer,
            animals lonely & hangry & near,
            animals with teeth, with gills, with gear, animals tailed &
            talented & fearful of the
            lugubrious & unrelenting night
in the image of the gone, the missed, the massive & least, the list,
            lust, dust & dawn, breath's
            wet work in the factories of desire & maps speculative &
            clear & the field you walked past on your way to school &
            the seeds in the field that knew another time, another
time, some other time, the gone, the going, the good
            goodbye
in the image of

THE CONCORD OF THE STRINGS

He blew harmonica and he was pretty good with that,
  but he wanted to play guitar.
                    —Son House on Robert Johnson

In November, it's hard to know
a cherry tree is a cherry tree.
If it has any leaves left, they're
raw as rust. The sound the wind
makes hustling through them's
a wolf whistle, what Emmett Till's
said to have done in Bryant's
Grocery Store. The second story's
fallen to Money mud. A magnolia
gives off a green heat between
two dilapidated buildings—inside
the vacant gas station it looks
like nothing's been touched
for decades but for forlorn fingers
of dust. In August of 1955 how
heavy were those lamps, the tree's
long bright white bulbs that are
a southern signature as ineluctable
as the creamy spit of cotton or
certain words we cannot say.

Some seventeen Augusts earlier
Robert Johnson sucked poison
and was planted, perhaps (at least
three gravesites claim him), under
a pecan tree just down the Money
road. His songs are sexy, secular
and we all know (or think we do)
his friendship with the devil, but

it's his own hand that scratched
these words etched on stone:
Jesus of Nazareth, King of Jerusalem
I know that my Redeemer liveth
and that He will call me from
the Grave.

            In "Preachin' Blues (Up
Jumped the Devil)" his picking's
as mean as money, faster than
the trains he often sang about.
His voice keens like mothers
in mourning, rasps, growls, shouts,
slows, picks up, accompanies his
playing, overpowers it & rests
as the strings say what they have
to say.

            I don't know why I say
these things, or if I have any right
to claim affliction, but I am burdened
by stories not my own
that tell me what my own stories mean
& a music sticks, & grows, & rages
like trees carrying, through winter's paucity,
the violence of spring.

OCTOBERSCAPE

Some days I think I could live inside Johnny Hartman's voice, its supple forlorn
abundance offering the sweet sadness of space to my lumped throat &
shuffled mind, slip into the long robes of his sullen baritone & watch autumn
comfortably, erotically unfold, e.g., a white pansy has emerged, without the
help or neglect of my thumbs, from a pot where an orchid no longer grows,
past & present overlapping, the one vanishing the other, time measured less
in the gentle exactness of Hartman's rendering of "September Song" than in
confounding elisions, like how he sings "September, November," as though the
luscious, meaty sorrow of the month between, all falling leaves & muted days, is
unbearable, not to be spoken or sung, to be hung in the closet with coats & hats
for lighter days, or colder, or maybe he simply forgot the month the way I can't
remember the time of year my father visited me in Brooklyn when I was sharing
an apartment with two girls I only half loved, the way I love most things, & after
a night of too much bourbon I brewed coffee in a French press & my father put
on the cd he'd bought the day before at Music Matters, *John Coltrane & Johnny
Hartman*, as we sat on the leather couch, the one with the cushions always sliding
out from under you the way time does when a song empties & augments you,
which is what people mean when they say something floored them, the coffee
was rich, it must have been October when the sky becomes a fine shampoo over
New York harbor & I was so young I had hardly been hurt by anything the way
Hartman's voice exquisitely bruised the air, the light was always soft in that
apartment, blocked by other buildings, or maybe it's only soft in my memory,
those rooms I keep opening in search of something, what was it, what is it about
the way he sings "the days grow short when you reach September" that bulldozes
me & of course it's not his voice I want to live inside but the shape & shift of that
month he cannot name, the one that flosses my modest breast even now, though
it is a different month in Texas than it was in New York or Vermont or Maryland
or Georgia, here the attenuation of nature is more im- than explicit, a state of
mind, the leaves barely blushing before they fall, stalks of corn tall as stanchions,
though come to think of it neither a voice nor a month is what I want but such
mellow hours with my father, or maybe not even that but for my affection to be
like a lung, receiving, expanding, filtering, returning, so that what is all around
me, the past, the air, the lone pear on a tree in need of company, I absorb, & what
is within me spools out into the day, the month, like breath, like a song where
the lyrics can't quite get to the heart of some loss because the days are glorious
but O they grow short.

On Learning Langston Hughes Wanted His Funeral to End with "Do Nothin' Til You Hear From Me"

Whether from catgut strung across
a span of steel or wind wounded
through wood or brass we all know
a sound that knows us, that calls
& claims each moment of our lives
even in death we want a groove
to soothe that passage mellow or
mournful or wild with the liquor
of love that drips down the chin
of a song until our knees knock
like the fuzz of bees brewing roses
at times the music dims, a melody
that once took the rug from under
us now makes it no further than
our ears our hearts can break only
so many times our legs dance with
abandon one minute the next are
shamed or sicknessed to stillness
but oh when a voice or violin hits
just so a note or notes the way
sunlight turns one body of water
into a thousand coins of shimmer
we are back in Kansas or wherever
first we knew or most we felt a
presence a shivering a freedom
from the cruel belt of history
of everything not music caught
in hoarse throats & stale feet
don't you want your life your
death even to sweat with singing?

MY GRANDFATHER'S RECORDS

When my grandmother died
my grandfather felt a need
to give away belongings
accumulated over countries
& decades as though the only
way to ward off loss was to lose.
So, pictures came off walls,
cups from cupboards, clothes
from cabinets. All the movies
they'd watched once or not
at all playable on devices
no longer available. Photos,
books, pots, pans. Little
lithographs from Japan.
I took a few of his records:
Jimmy Buffett's Christmas
carols, Lena sings the blues.
I'd never heard Billy Eckstine
before I let the needle caress
the double album bought
in New Orleans on their
honeymoon sixty years ago.
I becomes an envelope
when he sings *Everything*
I have is yours, love
a container, a multitude.
If two become one
in marriage what digit
does a widower bear?
Eckstine's voice syrups
my sadness, so I think

not just of her last days
when my grandmother's
hair, white, dried adrift
on her pillow, but what
dress she wore the night
they walked down Conti
to the Coliseum, where
for five dollars my grandfather
had bought two front-row
seats for *Mr. B* as friends
called the bandleader.
She had new perfume
behind her ears, her
skin became sunset
as the songs poured out
& my grandfather's
hand drifted from her
neck to spine to small
of back. They stood,
they swayed, the music
whiskey, their tolerance
high. A long night, dinner
before, drinks after, then
he watched her sleep,
the new day not yet at
the window, the days
after not yet recorded,
music without words, no strings.

Oral History of Silence

I woke in the wreck of history,
a slight sight in my seeing,

my body wet with what I guessed
was sweat but might've been blood.

They will know we are Christians
by our conquest. No, wait, that

isn't right. I keep getting things
wrong & wrong & wrong. It's how

I know I'm white. Well, well, well.
What I'm trying to say is, *sorry*.

I saw the Serra exhibit, behemoth
bones of rust. I saw
two black men carry spines
of steel to a dumpster. More

in trees, on streets. I saw white
men say this was normal, nothing
to get upset about. They were
sad they couldn't watch a nice

sport without thinking of justice
crying crying crying in cities
in the woods in the past. The past
keeps happening so often I've
decided to call it the future. I'm
reading the history of holiness.

It's a very frail book. I'm reading
a collection of apologies. I want
to be true to what I've seen, what
I've heard. For months I've sought
an appropriate vocabulary for prayer,
but everything feels false. I know for

the spider, silk is a lexicon of comfort,
but for the fly it is terror. I'm so afraid

my love language is silence.

TWO OF EVERYTHING

My house is two windows
with sheetrock in between.

Outside the windows
two cranes hold heaven

between their wings.
My heart is two varieties

of religious experience,
two wrongs, two rights.

Under my heart two
secrets will never see

the backside of the other,
unlike Noah's sons.

Shame & embarrassment
are two members of the

same family, cousins
who lick the salt in

the other's wound.
Now the two cranes

depart & with them
the world. Two days

until my father is drunk
again. You can save

Creation, but if you can't
hold your liquor, that, too,

will be remembered. It takes
two to linger, two to delve,

two to say what isn't there.
The cranes might be one.

Two hands cast a single shadow
on the wall that separates the windows.
My body is two: the one that
makes an S next to my beloved,

& the one that wanders the
aisles of Walmart muttering

what was it, what was it,
to everything that responds:

Made in China. My head
dwells in two worlds:

the imaginary, & the one
others tell me to believe.

I carry two Bibles:
one bound, one being.

When you sing, Augustine
is said to have said, *you pray*

twice. My prayers weigh half
the span of the cranes' lives.

Their feathers fracture water
into the ark of evening. Pleasure

is the half-sister of longing.
Two deaths play two songs

on my jukebox. The peach
tree where the cranes dance

goes by two names: what
we call her, & what she wants

to be called. The cranes
are quiet. Their quiet

doubles the way a heart,
broken in two, is also called love.

Birding

Then turned my head

as if to hear
more
closely

would make a difference.

As if hearing

more closely

might help

me to know

the song

the bird offered

to the dawn.

Once, I used to turn

that way
toward
a face
that turned

toward me.

As if seeing

more clearly
could keep
our love

from harm.

As if it was not harm

                    or the fear
                    of harm
                    that gave

our look

                    when I
                    when they

                                      turned

its electricity.

                    The power

of those dark

                    songs

                                    comes

even now to mind

                    the way
                    into the saxophone

                                  Charles Parker

swooped & turned

                    the curl of brass
                    into a cemetery
                    where flowers

                                  continue

to bloom

                    long after
                    they have

                                died.

ALL THINGS SEEN & UNSEEN

MAKER OF HEAVEN

Often it was just like the earth, but slower.
Having made everything that was, that would be, that might have been,
God, loves, was tired.
Sabbath, they said to the west wind. *Sabbath*, they wrote in the ink of oregano.
Sabbath the dead, the unborn, the real & what some thought was real but
      wasn't.
What God wanted was not quiet so much as the immaculate feeling that stills
      you
when you know something you have made has moved someone.
Bewilder, they tucked into the bellies of tangerines. *Bewilder*, the grapevine
      & the heavy luck of fermentation. *Bewilder*, the mouth of the ass & stars'
      speech.

When, suddenly,
on a Thursday evening as you press your tired head to the glass of the bus
      moving glacierly down Lexington Avenue past *Everything Must Go* signs &
      buskers offering their shattered delight to the harmonica's incessant need,
      a memory of the first time your tongue tasted the sugarsalt of inner thigh
      astonishes you with gleeful nostalgia,
a feeling so acute, so deliciously obliterating
you do not realize your breath has become a pant
until the gray-haired woman sitting in front of you turns to ask if you're
      alright,
her eyes adazzle with tender alarm,
her face wrinkled from years of such memories

      that

      that moment was made for you,
      & everything that kept you from & for that feeling,

mad

    & when the stairs of your bones flatten
    & all the names you've ever tongued are
        without mouths

    in heaven it is all preserved

Oh, what else, what else? Was there something
    else you wanted?
Just ask. Just ask.

This View of Life

Where the Croton empties out

                           into the Hudson

on the other side of trains'
musk not exactly autumn
but not exactly not, either,

                           twentysome swans

sung their gates which some call wings.

                           On a dead piece
of wood lingering in the water
a dark bird opened & closed its

                           parentheses.

What celebrities litter the glad
drift of dreams we call day.
There's grandeur, Charles Darwin wrote, *in this view of life.*

I ask, o now, for the space between the wild & the domestic
to diminish.

I ask for raisins in December.

                       Two wars take almonds from my cupboard.

Where will I find
my wool? A wound in the ear
is a wound entire.

                       Black swans leave West Point
to the dusk-done sky.

                                     Ossining

The world is fine without us
I can't help thinking
as I kneel before the altar of a honeysuckle bush
watch four bees sing
from the Hymnal of Late Summer.

I don't know why I return
so often to their company.
I suspect I like something
of their oblivious meanness,
their careless sweetness.

A week of rain to close
out the season, autumn's lustful
eye on all I have loved.
Those green leaves, light licking them
into late dusk. They will be reckoned.
Apples the color of sun in severest evening,
the ones I have brought to peel, to press.

Was it yesterday or months past
I sat under this sleeve of rust-rent
oak leaves & a year or a minute
ago I was so broken with need
I could not stitch one thought to
another only look & look at pollen
waiting to be put in its place we
are untransformed until our mouths
go into other mouths the dust
of roses not yet honey

Atlanta

Absolutely free & wild, Thoreau said, meaning
the world without human technologies,
meaning concert of warbler & wolf &
the fox sings sly sings slow sings *so long*.
                                    When no voice lathes
the Potomac   water slo-mo
                          July dissipated
my mind deeps & creeps,
                          crawls clear.
Ten minutes & I can't see
                          Snyder's Landing
shhh, shhh
              a paddle's the river's company & commentator.

Why is it so hard to be notsomeplaceelse?

Birds climb clouds the color of scratched script,

                  preserves of sound

What remains, I think, the name
of the Sally Mann exhibit I saw years ago
pictures of her dead dog's coat
the enormous landscapes of Antietam
two miles from where I now sit
taken on an antique camera blown
up, blurred, like the organs of the past
lifted from formaldehyded history
there are no people just the land
groaning where is your brother where
is your brother where is your brother
wide wings bring me back
and in the confusion of time & silhouette
I think *crane*   though I know this is not
the time for them.
Most of life, I once said to Andy, is mispronounced.
It's an eagle whose wings tremor
above the path that once connected the Chesapeake
to Ohio. O, o, summer's clarinet sounds so high & fine.
What concern to us are such things, A Kempis asked, *as genera & species?*

                                                    Sharpsburg

47

Jean-Nathan climbs
the bent branches
of the mango tree
knocks six green
globes to the ground
his pole a kind of pool-
stick this dangerous
delicious game. Rain
unspools perfume
from the high dark
hills. *Water, of course,*
supports long chains
of life: Rachel Carson.
Mosquitoes saw
a stagnant ditch. Disease
doesn't wait on Latin,
a name makes nothing
better, real.
Zoisseaux, Jean-Nathan
calls the crow inking
the gray sky. I ask
how to say "I love
what I smell."

Jolivert

We tear
        early pages
               from the atlas
                      to start a fire

One feels
        the strange
               ness Elizabeth
                      Bishop writes of Charles Darwin

sees the lone
        ly young man
               his eyes fixed on
                      acts and minute details

sinking or
        sliding giddi
               ly off into the un
                      known

We can only
        kiss
               in our mummy
                      sleeping bags

Morning
        frost every
               where is my
                      guide. Do not

harass the sal
        mon a sign
               commands I think
                      that's an eared grebe

fine as touch
        above the bare
               ly lit stream
                      but I'm usually wrong.

Salmon River

First Words

Who licked the caverns of
a certain fruit & said *apricot*,
heard a settling in a tree, uttered
turtledove, named the bird's
home *oak*, called a kind of
faith *principle*. I want to be
that bold, that clever, that free.
What would you contribute
to the sea of sound sitting between
two covers? Why *dictionary*?
Why not *lusterphony* or
harmonac? When a word
happens for the first time
we call it coining, the way
a face, a symbol is pressed
into precious metal, given
for a loaf of bread, a bit
of land. If you did not know
to call heaven *heaven* or
the weirdness that havocs
your heart *love*, what business
would dervish your mouth?
I envy beings without words,
the clover that doesn't have
to strain to recall the name
of its black-amber visitor
or say *sun* for the luxury
of light, or the cat who
laps (versatile word!)
the milk a cow has made
of grief & pasture. Silence,
dark river, invite me to your table.

WHAT FIRE WANTS TO SAY

When our friend died
we started to say things like
the last time we were all together
started to wear our hair over our eyes
started to leave lemon peels in ashtrays
we stopped shaving stopped making
collect calls late at night to cousins
in different time zones stopped
wearing the shirts he had worn
to clubs the smell of smoke
of patchouli a resin on the linen
a residue in our seldom hearts
we started to cut octopus into
tiny flowers & grill them black
over charcoal that felt like
little cymbals ready to burst
into music before we covered
them in kerosene a match no
match for what fire wants to
say to anyone who will listen
& anyone who won't stopped
drinking the recommended daily
amount started saying things like
remember when even when we
couldn't stopped going to the jail
just outside town where our friend
once worked before he took a job
defending real criminals I mean
people who don't go to jail
our friend had a nose he liked to say
was noble but we just called it
broken the way we feel now

WINTER IN ST. AUGUSTINE

for my grandmother, Marcena Kenney

1.

    Carolina chickadees checker Spanish moss
        with ribbons of flute-fine melody
    in the gray & golden almost-storm light
        that makes everything, even rotten
    lemons souring on brittle branches, luminous
        with possibility. Glad bags sag
    the ooze of Christmas dinner & last year's
        toys put out to make room for new
    ones heavy against their black coruscations.
        An Indian family slows to ask how
    many beaches lie ahead. The ocean—what
        has not been said of it? That its
    million-mollusk'd matrimonies of fin & spray,
        spit & craw overpower the poverty
    of the mind? Where else but from these
        foments of swept salt could we
    claim generation? Sea oats bend their green
        hair teased & blent in blue. The school
    for the deaf & blind where Ray Charles
        learned piano's off the island near
    my first love's home on Pine Street. A few
        blocks west in the summer of '64
    Andrew Young was beat on the head
        with a blackjack for making trouble
    in a white-run town. In "What'd I Say"
        Ray's fingers fly between white &
    black so fleet you're halfway back
        to Arkansas before he even gets
    to the line. The breakdown hovers between
        begging & betting his *hunhs*
    slow & long then fast & quick on the
        spumes of the Raelettes' waving

rejection & relent. Born in Albany just
        across town from my grandmother,
he shared her love of fresh strawberries.
        The way the sun ravishes a bowl
in her dining room, I figure he must be
        eating them in heaven.

2.

Recklessly

    the lemon tree

        buds pink

through the night.

    Through the afternoon

        light lavishes

a pale cement wall,

    nine swallows swim

        out of bare poplars.

Recklessly

    little purple flowers

        the size of thorns

jet out of the blood

    dark coleus. We

        redeem ourselves

in birdsong. Sweetness

    in the slowness.

        The circles of the onion,

Egyptians thought,

    imitated the concentric

        universe. You slip

a leaf of butter

    into a pan, watch

        its slow descent

like a bather risking

    a toe, an ankle

        to the steaming water

you tear a dozen

    leaves of basil

        toss them next to

odd ears of onion

of cooking, your cool

cutting board to glass

Recklessly

a mile or two from

that some argue

When do we ever

The poorest hole

town dearer to me

rice. Years before

for a girl's off-blonde

in the white wind.

to speak her language.

pop, pop, pop

hands glide

of Gruner. What have

a loon landed next

where Audubon painted

was really Greater

know what we're

in the Creation

than any where

I learned the names

hair. The loon cannot

A family comes to help

I love the resistance

from spice rack to

we done to earn the world?

to waves crashing

his Greenshanks

Yellowlegs.

looking at?

he called this

I learned to kiss, cook

of any birds, buds

raise gray arms

her. They're trying

I am a bird.

3.

Someday I'll die here, under a palm tree
growing right up the middle of a live oak.
Nature has never been my nature,
though I know a robin's cry, a wren.
I keep a glass of sea oats by my bed.
Nobody knows whether Ponce de Leon
named the state for the Easter season
or flowers he saw as he approached the shore.
It is a pretty name, though, isn't it? Florida.
Those will be the waters that calm and claim
my wrestling, wrestled pulse. So many sunsets
watched, so many books strewn with sand.
My life is reading by a window. Strange
that some rooms are like cages. I am brushing
the walls, I am looking for a lighter coat.

WHAT IT MEANS TO BE COLD

The world loves to make you sad.

April snow, the gas company threatens to disconnect service.

> You are nine years old next to the Gulf of Mexico,
>   your father speaks of love.

Now when you see the ocean you think it is love,
& when you see your lover
you wish you could drown,

because your breath is useless,
your body a shell,
a sound the ocean makes far from the ocean
a feeling of love far from love.

> You are sixteen years old in the Atlantic Ocean
>   with the first girl you kiss.

Now when you drive into St. Augustine you remember
the way the salt air took
                 your breath by surprise,
the way her tongue was one language
& her nipple another
& you will never be that fluent again
because language is a kind of wind
                 & you are a kind of grass
& bees do not know the difference between capitalism & socialism.

In one old photograph your eyes are level with the counter.
You were that small, once, you are that small, still.
& the light from whatever forgotten afternoon that was
surrounds the side of your face like workers gathered outside a factory,
         which is their factory, because they work there

                & which is not their factory, because they do not own it.

Four days before Easter.

                    What difference does it make if you eat lamb
                          or vegetables?
                    What does a nail feel like in your flesh &
                        coming out of your flesh?

Before he died, Jesus told his disciples they would have to love everyone.

Jesus is not the ocean, or the page, or my father. He is not a word, or a language,
                                  or a wind.

He is the image inside the imagination.
                  He is fruitful, & multiplies, the way language does,
        the way the ocean does, the way the flowers of my imagination
                        become the flowers of my garden,
           which become the flowers of my past,
                          & the past is where love lives
& love is my rusted old Honda Accord, which is the shortest distance
                between Hagerstown & St. Augustine,

which is the line
that connects
my breath
to my body,
which is a kind
of ocean, all
it ever wants
is to love everyone.

                Fireflies dance in the summer field
                            of my past.
They are the first thing I remember,
an early language, a swimming.

                The water is cold. I cannot breathe. My blood is blue.

If someone from Atlanta tells you

                          not to buy Coca Cola

    will you shoot him

           in the face on a balcony in Memphis?

Spring murders the daffodils of my imagination.

           It takes their yellow heads & hangs them on the wind.

White lilies mean you are forgiven.

                     Cold water means love will live again.

How much of your life are you willing to put on the line?

          How much winter keeps your heart

                            in spring?

In Gethsemane can you hear the ocean,

                 which is your father

who speaks of love.

Maker of &

& alphabets of ocean's forlorn
& your sister you speak to every morning & the silence in your speech
& the yarn she carries in her bag made by hands smaller than sleep
& the knitting of your mother's womb
& fever blisters
& the time it takes to boil water
& the river the cloud the cloud the river the cloud the river the river
& public libraries
& private libraries
& libraries of skin & song & silk & sweets
& Tokyo
& Toledo
& cans in basements of hoarders
& caviar's exquisite calligraphy
& the sun voracious & endless except for when it ends
& what you thought you wanted
& what you were afraid to ask
& your grandmother's handwriting
& the arthritis that elongated her ss
& Dolly Parton
& your ears' ellipses
& tents where families without work sleep
& master building plans of churches across overpasses from tent cities
& gangrene
& cries heard & unheard
& Spanish Steps
& calls to prayer
& atheists
& the pencils made by Henry Thoreau
& Thoreau's unpublished erotica
& galaxies

& snails who speak neither French nor butter & parsley
& flamingoes' oratorio
& hydroelectric power
& dams & engineers & erosion & drought
& Georgia O'Keeffe's brushes, each hair, each pigment, a praise, a prairie
& sorcery of morel chanting, *hear ye, hear ye*
& gauze that says to blood, *there there*
& the temple of the watermelon, dripping stained glass
& trees consumed in fire & trees that hung bodies like laundry, & trees that
     will be planted tomorrow & tomorrow & trees that take their tiny fingers,
     & count & count & count then declare persimmons!
& the writers of Exodus & the livers of Exodus & Bob Marley & the Wailers
& the readers of Exodus & its midrash
& the bellies of words, scratched to ecstasy
& Charles Darwin & the Galapagos Islands & tourists of evolution & eugenics
& every pepper & the sauces they hot
& fjords & Ford & Robert McNamara & the million killed by his brilliance
& blossoms blossoms blossoms promiscuous in spring
& yeast & salt & flour & egg & carraway
& Virgil & his translators & Sappho & hers
& peony
& mollusk
& maybe
& Van Gogh's sunflowers & starry nights & sowers & sore
& the iron of Lucille Clifton, its wild steam
& afternoon's abattoir
& goose & gander
& all the poets drinking cooling green tea & reading Mary Oliver's "Wild Geese"
& presidents dead & queens dead & prime ministers dead & everyone without
     title or biography dead & the living dead
& the Ozarks & the Andes & the Catskills & all the rivers in that John Ashbery
     poem
& the television show *The Jeffersons* & Thomas Jefferson & Sally Hemings
& animals extinct & insects & the tongues of spiders
& Basho & Li Po & Cardi B & Ye
& arugula & radicchio & endive
& kingfishers & carolina wrens & cuckoos & Audubon's incorrigibility
& the cold sweat James Brown woke up in & the bad suit he was buried in

& the bodhi tree & the numinous & Nirvana & the last tree Kurt Cobain saw
& seesaws & slides & swings
& newts & lizards & salamanders & toads & alligators & snakes
& pimento cheese & bourbon & overbred horses
& all the covers of The Rolling Stones' "Wild Horses"
& Italy & Little Italy & China & Chinatown & the clothes Jack Nicholson wore
    in the 1970s
& every -onomy & -ology & -osophy
& coal miners & their daughters & all the opries grand & ole
& big cities & little cities & ghost towns & pueblos & ruins & the villages of
    moles & gophers
& grass & grass & grass
& the brain wider than the sky
& the sky
& Earth, Wind & Fire
& September & all the months & the moon
& the cello with her memories of bliss
& all the children of Johann Sebastian Bach, his shoes & cantatas
& Billie Holiday's lovers & gloves
& the harps & saxophones of the Coltranes
& fingernails & toenails & salons
& Blue Ivy & Beyoncé & Solange
& syrah & mourvedre & grenache
& waiting & wanting & panting & thumbing
& dizziness & daring & dread & duende
& the Grand Canyon & all canyons who feel inadequate by comparison
& humiliation & adoration & anonymous art
& the names flowers give one another
& the affection of bees
& hollow
& holy
& hello
& how
& water seethed into the ceremony of ice
& this moment & this & this & this
& palms become ash to remind you you're dust
& the body of Christ broken for you

THE BODY OF CHRIST

TACOS

i.m. Anthony Bourdain, 1956–2018

The red sauce is hot af the guy at the table
      next to mine declares to no one
in particular though he's there with a woman
      more interested in her feed than him.
It's ten in the morning on a Saturday,
      everyone else still in bed
or not getting paid enough for the work
      they're doing. I pour red &
green over my migas until the eggs
      vanish. I want my mouth a fire,
a ruined village, a place tourists will
      walk through later shaking
their heads asking themselves & the guide
      what happened? Which is what
I keep asking as I look at the man with
      an accordion strapped to his chest,
his hair black as loss & mirroring wholly
      the sun. He's waiting for the bus
on Pleasant Valley to take him home or
      some midmorning gig. I can't
see his face but I know what it looks like.
      It's beautiful & heavy with capitalism
& astonishment. A face not strange to
      sorrow, to standing over caskets.
The keys on his instrument gleam like
      flowers waiting to be cut. As
I devour my tacos I recognize the truth
      in my teeth, taproot of this
mortal coil: some tastes will never
      go away, some words will

never be enough. The musician's leather
      jacket bears an angel on its
back, her slender, Marian figure folded
      in wings or flames I don't know.
I don't know. Whatever song she sings
      she sings for you.

EUCHARIST

I want the world in my mouth.
Walnut, avocado, nasturtium.
Icewine, edelweiss, dictionary.
Can you swallow sunset?
I'll try.
Himalayan salt, & Morton's.
Disappointment, exhilaration, hope.
Lake Michigan, the Gulf of Mexico.
The body of Christ, the bread of heaven.
Sometimes in my motley desire
I've put things there
that didn't belong.
An older actor's nipple, wanting
to please, to play a part.
Words I did not mean,
or did not know the meaning of.
Lips I thought I wanted
or I thought wanted me.
Sweet, sour, bitter, blessed.
O Master, will I ever be slaked?

Host

i.m. Jake Adam York, 1972–2012

Well it's March so the cherry
            trees submit slender peppermint flowers
     for our consideration
each turn in weather
an invitation not
     to neglect
        to marvel
     I wonder why the words   cherry blossom
         so sway
            so sway me
or when you first knew
        you would host in poems
            a cast of forgotten martyrs
    their afternoons & clothing & smoked meats & final hours
          line after line
pulling us back to Mississippi
       to Alabama
            to Georgia in the 1950s
what it felt like to be
       black there or white
    but who
         is host & who is guest
            what causes
             Spanish moss
I ask three months after you've died at Greenfield Lake
Ashley says
         it's a parasite
how can something so nasty be so lovely
        I think of Walt who saw
     a live oak in Louisiana & was put in mind of manly love
            & took some

moss home to consider to remember to feel

                                              the place he no longer was

the last time I was in New Orleans I saw

                            Alison Saar's *Travelin' Light*

      a sculpture patterned after Japanese temple bells

                         but the bell

is a man

           hanging

                        from his feet

                                      the moss above

a kind of shroud   the whole sky   a cave   that cannot keep him

                      dead

      no one to see, Billie's menthol-sugar voice trembles, *I'm free*
as the breeze,

              the 'ee' stretches, bends vicious,
no one but me, she digs the personal pronoun like it's dark

                        earth covering who knows

    what
& my memories,

                that great subject—or project?—we take

    or does it take us

                like the bread Augustine said
will not change me into you like the food your flesh eats,
but you will be changed into me

Hymn

Some of the things I wasn't doing at the age of 22:
learning the Latin names of flowers (or even their English ones)
living abroad, recording music with the intensity & abandon
you hear on every single cut
of *At Last!* on which Riley Hampton's orchestra's
a tame & obliging brook under storm-spew'd sheets
of Jamesetta Hawkins'—I hesitate to apply so diminutive
a word as *voice* to what heaves, careens, flutters & screams
from that beautiful black body that came to be known
like so many other beautiful black bodies
by her first name only—Billie, Ella, Dinah, Nina, Etta—
just to slip the tongue around those two syllables,
silk gloves tailored to contain exactly what they need & nothing
more, is to loose a world, a wonder, a wound
healed only by the implacable keeling
that overcomes the strings within the first 2 seconds
of "Anything to Say You're Mine"
& gets so deep inside the body
it is no wonder we sing hymns
let certain words, certain sounds touch
the ribs, the hips, the feet, the teeth—
an utmost possession & discipline—
when Paul said the Spirit intercedes
with sighs too deep for words
he must have had in mind a wracked wail
such as churns from Etta & turns the simple pronoun "I"
into a four-measure lament, an unspeakable
only singable & singeing cry over the gulf
between the soul & what the soul longs for—
night hangs heaven-festered scents

of jasmine & geranium across the street
from the Pentecostal church I walk by on my way
to the bus past a cherry, a magnolia tree
bewitched into flower
there is no way to know the time
of God's music but the ink-blotted moon moans, moans.

BLACKCHURCH

After many years of fruitless quest
for what I thought was love but
know now to be vanity, vanity my middle-
name & patrimony, vanity my mirror &
rhythm section, I went, vain & unrepentant,
into a tabernacle most hallowed in this place
called Tis-of-Thee, liberty illusion & myth,
quilt passed generationally as other hereditary
illnesses & whatnot. For when a
limbstrewn wanderluster in seek of salve
gets to some dead end & says, *Oh, let me
live*, pity that fool & hasten him to King's
home, spiritual & literal, Ebenezer up
the street from the 2-story Victorian
where, A.D. 1929 in the disaster aka
America, came of a woman a man who,
having spoken over years, from depths still
plumbless, with the sort of timbre & cadence
vouchsafed O surely to the elect alone, was
thanked for his witness with a bullet in the face.
Friends, think me not ignorant that
such recompense has been tendered
again & again & again & again, but,
I confess, that morning, when Spirit
said, Visit ye my historic Blackchurch,
I was, to put it mildly, dumb. Hark,
it's been my privilege whitely to walk
wherever my bodymind cares to go,
with little thought but wherever *there*
be, hence my satisfaction. O,
I was not, whiteboy though I am,

without deprivation, for on that very
day my bodymind did brood, did brood,
yes, lovelies, in my solemn heart there
had a wreck occurred. What herons,
what swans in seasons past had idled
in parks dear to me had fled. I say
I was a mess. So wrought, so
done, I turned, unwitting, toward redemption
I could not name nor earn, but under the
choir's caress, in the carrel where many
an earnest student of the Word had asked
How long, O Lord, I felt move over me,
within me, a fire that some have named
YHWH, some history, some, bless them,
have said is nothing but the random congress
of synapses, a molecular procedure no
more meaningful than sunset or horseshit.
Well, friends, I can only assure you that
having seen the Sistine & like manner
of murals, & in consideration of Coltrane,
& the bus vernacular of a Missus Rosa
Parks, & after some years allowing Bach's
Passions to destroy me, as well as the
avenuewide voice of Mahalia Jackson,
in addition to the sermons preached
but twenty blocks from where whitely
I resided the better part of Obamayears,
it is my glad conclusion, despite ample
evidence of cruelty, disintegration, &
the relentless belltolling that tells me
more & more to dust have returned,
that God is real for I can feel Them
in my soul. & so I commit my vanities
& shortcomings to that limbly business,
Church, believing, for all my trespasses
& stupidities, Love may, yet, have the final
　　　Word.

CLOSING IN

More & more needles fall from the pines.
Everywhere symbols, if that's your thing.
To live always in the possible, to urge
your flesh to be as keen as melons softening
on summersad vines. I am tired of everything
that isn't lovely. I am tired of the way my
shoulders hoard stress, stacks & stupid stacks.
Everybody's an expert in somebody else's
business. I do not want to be any busier
than my basil plant, swallowing the sun,
the soil, the errant water. We suppose we
know a thing or two about botany, about
the intelligence of leaf, stem, root. Have you
noticed the way plants lean, as though longing
for news from a neighbor, a song, a touch, just
a little touch. It has been
a hard season for bodies, for the given
strangeness of care. Even now, the kind
music of a lark lingering in the crape myrtle
has something bereft about it. Like a whistle,
moving through lips, sounds going &
coming, the desirer closing in on the desired.

ANNUNCIATION

Even after we'd watched them, the women
with hair darker than the city's night sky will
ever again be, make tortillas—mixing, pressing,
waiting (for what art on earth is not at least
half waiting)—we still did not comprehend
what had been done, much like our neighbor's
cat, years ago, kept moving a mound of
fur around the yard as though that motion
would revive her kitten. *Let it be with me*
according to your word, Mary said when
a strange man showed up & offered
absurd promises, as strange men often make.
She could have been, perhaps should have been
mistrustful. Instead she turned to song,
meadow of sound sown with awe, & the space
between the light outside her body, & the light
inside her body, vanished. Maybe it was
the pitcher of margaritas we drank as we
tried to learn the secrets of salsa in that cooking
class we'd won in a raffle we couldn't remember
entering, maybe it was the way the women called
each of us *sweetheart*, the two syllables savored
as though they were also part of the recipe.
Whatever caused my friend to divulge a story
he'd never shared with anyone, not even his mother
disappearing in a hospice bed in Houston,
had the anonymous splendor of angels, showing up
sometimes in books you know so well you can recite
the unwritten parts, sometimes in restaurants
on the gentrifying edge of town, always
with the awful force of love.

NEITHER ON THIS MOUNTAIN
NOR IN JERUSALEM

Where the pond no longer hidden by reeds
keeps moonlight as though for some future banquet

I once heard a woman laughing with such abandon
it could have only meant two things: it was summer,

or she had been loaded with loss after loss after staggering
loss, the way a balloon, overfilled, bursts into a giggle

of air. When I approached her, I realized it was my own
laughter that wrecked the quiet. It was winter. My body

had not made room for the delight of travelers or their
insatiable eyes fastened upon the loaves that weighed

down my father's table. There is a church in the walnut tree
& a church in the eyes of dead trout. My mother's

womb: a church. The children I'll not bear: a choir.
The rooms where I wait for dawn: a psaltery.

The woman, startled by my laughter, explained
something in a language I don't know. The sound

distant traffic makes. The sound time turns into flesh
& woodmusic. Darkness gives to dark & worries

the light. Light trembles in churches & the salted
organs of bathers. Water minus water yields want.

I'm thirsty, the woman said with my mouth. What was
worse, the way I wanted to satisfy her, or the way I didn't.

THE DISTANCES

Tomorrow I will move a fig tree
from its pot to the sandy ground
The day after I will set elements
upon my tongue: salt, water, yeast,
clove. For months I've watched
transformations wordless & disturbed.
I don't follow the zodiac but I know
my sign. Right, left, up, down.
We haven't sufficient words for the distances we encounter, so we settle on these:
prairie, mountain, missing, moon. *I relieved your shoulder of the burden*, a psalmist
said. Yesterday I lifted a woman into her car: smell of frailty on my hands. How many
seasons have the seeds I've spoken to the rude dirt said nothing, nothing. How many
states have I visited museums memorializing massacres. In childhood I could not have
known my obsession with dusk was a flirtation with finitude. Finishing is overrated
if sometimes necessary. My drawer accumulates unsent letters the way someone
who hasn't had a proper meal in days will settle for scraps. Each word written is
wed to one that stays inside the pen,
the mind a furrow of silence. How
do you do, I ask the spruce in our
sporadic correspondence. She
responds in jay, in owl. Howls
are like bowls the soul pours
its soup in. The first time I saw
someone die I thought their breath
was a wizard, but nothing was
behind the curtain. Spring's
relentless with comforts, salve
on each wound winter opened,
salted. We do not have much
further, my grandfather used to
say, regardless of map's testimony.
Each time he lost someone his
smile became a country with stricter
border security. Let go, let go
the ocean told him. *My burden
is easy*, Jesus said. Oh really?
What, then, is this weight
upon my shoulders, my god?

NEAR THE END

On a hill near a house where I used to live
an olive tree hosted a congregation of starlings.
Murmuration, I guess they're called, when
they gather, just as there is, I'm sure, a word
for the way the sun, in August, italicized
the olives, until the ones on the tree & the ones
in our mouths were indistinguishable. I don't
think I'd call what the birds did murmuring,
but then I often say something for the satisfaction
of its sound & worry about the meaning later.
When I lived there, near that hill, I hardly
worried at all. If I did, it was over what
to wear, how to talk to a girl whose skin murmured
see me, see me. We went to the old theater
on Key Street to see *Late August, Early September*.
There's a scene near the end—I think it's near
the end—in which a girl stands outside a club,
Stereolab murmuring onto the sidewalk. Waiting
for her lover, she doesn't know he has died.
Just as there was a time when I didn't yet know
you had died. I go there in my mind, the way
the starlings returned to the olive tree after
it had been cut down to make way for custom homes, the future.

AT A BURGER KING NEAR I-35
ON THE NEXT-TO-LAST DAY OF THE YEAR

Luke 2:8-20

Far from here, where earth's flat & featureless
as the men I sit among to eat my Whopper, families of cows
wander from grass to grass, unremembering, their slaughter
hours or days in the future. The hospitable sun shines
on their black backs, the wind shimmies as their tails toss at what
flies the cold hasn't killed. December hunches into bodies
the way my friend's grandmother, after her husband of seventy years died,
leaned toward everyone who approached her, craving consolation.
Her sobs sound still in my heart, making pasture there.
Are the ones who care for these cows, milking & readying them
for market, cursing them & gazing with love into their ponderous dark eyes,
so different from the shepherds who waited chapped & without name
for the angels' bop to startle them to Bethlehem? Imagine
Mary & Joseph, dazed by travel, harassment, & the liquor of birth,
their boy small, swaddled, aghast with winter's real, as they look up
to see a group of migrant farmworkers whose lips, usually tight
with the fret of wages & their careless charges, burst into the juice
of music, *Glory to God*. How they must have smelled, hands
acquainted with the untheological functions of earth & her animals,
their hair sordid halos above faces parsed by fear & scorn.
The stable, unremarkable in its squalor, permitted, then,
such joy as I suppose enters the minds of the dying when, no longer
cognizant of the people at their bedside, they begin to see
familiars lost decades prior. *Through a glass darkly*,
one hope-glutted witness would write, & I want to hold
a mirror before each shepherd, each soul who picks
the red disks that ooze over every patty of beef that gives me
a sliver of delight, so I can see what strangers walked
so long to see there, on the outskirts of town, in a child:
a day, a new day, the very dazzle of dawn
broken over the whole damn world.

How to Make a Meal

Strike the little lamb on the back of the head.
Claw, cleave into
the bloodrich shoulders
& let the red rinse fragrance the softly seasoned air.
Tear from the bleated body swirling calligraphy of fur,
each strand a rebuke to the fuss of taxidermy.
What is flesh but the cunning music of God,
the culmination of light's long lament & lamination?
Once you get to rib & kidney,
the useless generous heart,
make fine cuts so that those with little
appetite can get a taste.
You will need to find
a reliable reservoir of salt.
Sticks of cinnamon, the churn of butter, the chant of onion.
If bread is your prayer, make plenty of it.
If wine is your prayer, forgive those who cannot drink, out of modesty or
　　　madness.
Decorate a table long enough for head to hoof with emblems
of what you've been led to believe correspond with the Eternal.
Think of everything the lamb ever took
sweet & stupid into his unorthodox mouth. Thank it.
Then, when you feel almost too exhausted even to sit,
invite the ones who've humiliated you to a plate,
those whom you've said, in secret, such petty & unpretty things about.
What can you do, given famine & fortune,
the rich endless array of hunger, but eat.

NOTES

Many of the poems in this collection are informed by the ancient practice of midrash, a way of reading sacred texts that wonders what stories exist around, beneath, and behind the primary texts. My understanding of midrash is primarily owed to the work of Avivah Gottlieb Zornberg. I recommend her books on Torah and midrash enthusiastically. Poems which feature a scripture notation under their titles are not necessarily midrashic, but they are in conversation with those verses.

SPIES
Stone Mountain, just east of Atlanta, was carved by Gutzon Borglum, the sculptor of Mt. Rushmore, to commemorate leaders of the confederacy. The park surrounding it was opened to the public on the 100th anniversary of Abraham Lincoln's assassination, and the area has long been a bastion of the Ku Klux Klan.

J. Edgar Hoover in particular and the FBI in general were relentless in their efforts to discredit the character and ministry of the Rev. Dr. Martin Luther King Jr. See David Garrow's *The FBI and Martin Luther King, Jr.*

ON THE OTHER SIDE OF ROBERT E. LEE
As in many cities throughout Texas, Austin has named many streets after confederate leaders. The street that runs just east of Barton Springs has subsequently been renamed. Draylen Mason was a high school student planning to attend the University of Texas on a music scholarship. A gifted player of the double bass, Mason was killed in 2018 when he opened a package containing a pipe bomb planted by Mark Anthony Conditt.

PHILADELPHIA
One of the first places Ronald Reagan spoke as he launched his 1980 presidential campaign was Philadelphia, Mississippi, where in 1964 three Civil Rights workers were kidnapped and brutally murdered. In his speech, Reagan paid lip service to states' rights, a frequent talking point of neo-confederates who wish to disguise or minimize the brutality of enslavement in American history.

Imago Dei

At a lunch meeting of the National Book Award committee in 1950, Wallace Stevens used a racist epithet to ask about the identity of someone in a photograph; it was Gwendolyn Brooks.

The Concord of the Strings

Emmett Till was murdered in Money, Mississippi in 1955. Nearby is a gravestone marking the final resting place of the great blues guitarist Robert Johnson, though several others in the vicinity claim that distinction.

This View of Life

What Remains was the name of an exhibit of Sally Mann's photographs concerned with death. There is a monograph of the exhibit from 2003 published by Bulfinch. Mann took the title from a line by Ezra Pound: "What thou lovest well remains."

Winter in St. Augustine

St. Augustine, Florida was one of the first European colonies in North America. In the 1960s it was a pivotal site in the Civil Rights movement. Dr. King and his colleagues would go for vacation to a beach just south of the town, and their presence frequently generated violence from KKK members and sympathizers. Ray Charles spent part of his childhood at a school near the Spanish fort. John James Audubon was another (unimpressed) visitor to the area.

What It Means to Be Cold

The final speech Dr. King made, on April 3, 1968 at the Mason Temple in Memphis, Tennessee, called for a boycott of numerous companies in an effort to achieve further civil rights. He was assassinated at the Lorraine Motel the following evening.

Host

Jake Adam York was working on a poetry project that spanned several collections when he suffered a stroke and died at the age of forty. He gave the title *Inscriptions for Air* to the overall project, which memorialized the martyrs of the US Civil Rights movement.

Alison Saar is an American sculptor whose artwork focuses on the African diaspora and Black female identity. The title for the work referenced derives from the Billie Holiday song of the same name.

HYMN
Jamesetta Hawkins was the birthname of Etta James.

BLACKCHURCH
Ebenezer Baptist Church was founded in 1886 by John A. Parker. In 1894 Adam Daniel Williams became pastor, and his grandson, the Rev. Dr. Martin Luther King Jr., was serving, with his father the Rev. Martin Luther Sr., as co-pastor at the time of his assassination in 1968. I was a member of the church from 2008–2013 and served on the pastoral staff from 2011–2013.

A NOTE ON THE COVER ART
I got to know the extraordinary Lanecia Rouse Tinsley in her role as artist-in-residence at Holy Family Episcopal Church HTX, where I have enjoyed my first assignment as an Episcopal priest. Holy Family commissioned a series of paintings from Lanecia that explore the liturgical seasons and rites of the church. The painting on the cover is her baptism parament, which hangs above Holy Family's font. On Sundays after the sermon, the congregation gathers around the font to say together the prayers of the people and the Nicene Creed. "We believe in God the Father, the maker of heaven & earth . . ." This painting has a cosmic intensity and beauty that captures both creation and the rebirth the church affirms through the rite of baptism. I cannot think of another painting that better expresses visually what I am exploring in these poems, and am grateful to Lanecia and Holy Family for sharing it with us.

ACKNOWLEDGMENTS

Something I love about the Nicene Creed (from which this book's title comes)—such as we recite it in the Episcopal church—is the plurality of the speaking subject. *We believe.* Belief is never singular, it's communal, and so is a book. This collection of poems is, in many ways, a palimpsest and portmanteau that has evolved over twenty years out of countless encounters with other poems, other people, the places and beings that have enriched my life and shuddered into urgent expression.

To my family, I owe you so much. My grandmother, Marcena Kenney. Your own love of books and writing shaped me, even when your hopes were that I might pursue something more lucrative than poetry. My grandfather, Howard Kenney, your generosity has been a model, as has your enthusiasm for church and culture. Larry Myers, my father and friend, for all the ways you have fostered my love of quiet places, dark skies, deep conversations, and good books, I'm appreciative beyond measure. Cheryl Kenney, my mother and favorite patron of the arts, you have instilled from my infancy a devotion to everything made well, from meals to movies, clothes to books, and everything in between. For all you've given me, thanks. To my aunts, uncles, and cousins, I'm grateful for all the love, kindness, and laughter over the years. Gratitude to my family through marriage: Hank and Jackie Blum, Momlynn, Leslie Massad, Betsy and Larry Roadman. I'm so lucky to have you all in my life.

To the teachers who over several decades instigated and cultivated my delights and obsessions in storytelling and language's many gleams and oddities, you are the core of these pages. I thank especially those writers who patiently encountered my roughest drafts and taught me by example: Joan Selby, Tony Eprile, April Bernard, Roland Merullo, Edward Hoagland, Mary Oliver, Sharon Olds, Philip Levine, Yusef Komunyakaa. For those who have seen something in my work since, I am indebted, with special thanks to Campbell McGrath, Jericho Brown, Carrie Fountain, and Li-Young Lee.

To the friends who have showed up at readings and asked for copies and raised glasses and looked at drafts, from Bennington to now: Marcos Barbery, Alyssa Lowe, Chris Zubryd, Hailey Higdon, Andrew Hughes, Sarah Boardman, Whit Griffin, Elaine Fletcher Chapman, Colin Cheney, Janine Joseph, Jessica Ratigan, Genessa Georgi, Ashley Wilson, Tim Moore, Julie Bloemeke, Ginger Murchison, Emily Schulten, Dionne Irving, Melissa Range, Austin Segrest, Judith Winfrey, Kyle Schlesinger, Tess Taylor, Brynn Saito, Ashunda Norris. I carry you in my heart and in these pages.

For the extraordinary dedication to the life of literature and explorations of art emanating out of ecology and theology, I cannot sufficiently express how grateful I am to my *EcoTheo Review* people: Crystal Oliver, Han VanderHart, Esteban Rodríguez, Alexandria Barbera, Matt Burgess, Wayne Johns, Sharon Yao, Carter Boyd, Maria Judnick, Ajanae Dawkins, Michelle Kim Hall, Julie Wan, Veronica Schorr, JC Niala, Kiki McGrath, Megan Adams, roame jasmin, Veronica Schorr. To the rest of the EcoTheo family: Anastacia Renee, Natalie Graham, Spencer Reece, Eugénie Bisulco, Cynthia Kittredge, Roger Reeves, Allison Seay, Devon Abts, Anya Backlund, Carrie Fountain, Shann Ray—love and mille grazie. My Brother, my comrade in poetry and priesting, Travis Helms. Gratitude eternal.

For the gift of your art, Lanecia Rouse Tinsley, thank you. It's such a joy to have this painting as the cover of my first book. Thanks to my Holy Family family, especially Jacob Breeze and Chap Edmonson. I've enjoyed many church homes and faith families during the years I worked on this book, and have been formed, held, and buoyed by the people of Ebenezer Baptist Church, Candler School of Theology, Holy Comforter, Church of the Common Ground, All Saints', Calvary, and St. James'. Special thanks to Raphael Warnock, Luther Smith, Brent Strawn, Luke Timothy Johnson, Noel Erskine, Mike Tanner, Mary Wetzel, Geoffrey Hoare, Noelle York-Simmons, Lisa Burns, Lisa Saunders, and Eileen O'Brien.

Thank you, Casie Dodd, for your faith in this collection of poems. It's an honor to be part of Belle Point Press.

To my partner and favorite person, Allison Grace Myers, you have sustained me as this book has come to be. If it or I am any good it's a credit to your love, creativity, and generosity. To our son, Robinson, the heart outside my heart. You inspire these poems and more.

Gratitude to the editors, readers, and supporters of the following journals in which some of these poems originally appeared, often in different form: *Barrelhouse, The Believer, Copper Nickel, DIAGRAM, Diode, Hampden-Sydney Poetry Review, Harvard Divinity Bulletin, Image, Kenyon Review, New Orleans Review, North American Review, The Paris Review, Prairie Schooner, RHINO, Southern Indiana Review, Trinity House Review.*

"Spies" appeared in *The Familiar Wild: On Dogs & Poetry* (Sundress Publications), edited by Ruth Awad and Rachel Mennies.

Jason Myers serves as editor-in-chief of *EcoTheo Review* and co-director of EcoTheo Collective. A National Poetry Series finalist, he lives with his family on the lands of the Coahuiltecan peoples and is a priest in the Episcopal Diocese of Texas. This is his first collection of poems. *A Place for the Genuine: Reflections on Nature, Poetry, and Vocation* will be published by Eerdmans in 2024.